Low Calorie
COOKBOOK

Low Calorie Cookbook is also published under the title *Light Menus*.

This cookbook is one of a series of limited edition hardcover cookbooks. Other books in the series include:

Budget Saving Meals Cookbook
Casseroles and One-Dish Meals Cookbook
Chicken and Poultry Cookbook
Grill and Barbecue Cooking
Ground Meat Cookbook
Guide to Microwave Cookbook

Hershey's ® Chocolate and Cocoa Cookbook
Lunch and Brunch Cookbook
Old-Fashioned Family Cookbook
Soup, Salad and Sandwich Cookbook
Wok Cookbook

For more information on and a full description of any of the Ideals cookbooks listed above, please write:
Ideals Cookbooks
P.O. Box 148000
Nashville, TN 37214-8000

Ideals Publishing Corp.
Nashville, Tennessee

Contents

Published by Ideals Publishing Corporation
Nelson Place at Elm Hill Pike
Nashville, Tennessee

Cover Photo:
Stir-Fry Pasta Primavera, page 41

Swiss Cheese Soup, page 18

Menus for Brunch

Mexican Breakfast
Orange Papaya Smoothie

Mexican Breakfast

Makes 4 servings

2 teaspoons safflower oil
1 small red onion, chopped
½ green pepper, seeded and diced
2 12-ounce jars salsa
8 eggs, lightly beaten
¼ cup sliced jalapeño peppers

1 tablespoon butter *or* margarine
4 large corn tortillas
½ cup grated medium Cheddar cheese
Sliced green onion
Sliced jalapeño peppers
Chopped fresh cilantro *or* parsley

Heat oil in medium saucepan. Sauté onion and green pepper in oil. Add salsa and simmer, uncovered, about 10 minutes. Remove sauce from heat. In a bowl, mix eggs and jalapeños. In a large skillet melt butter *or* margarine over medium heat. Scramble egg mixture in butter *or* margarine until eggs are cooked but still moist.

Dip tortillas in salsa mixture until soft. Spoon ¼ of the scrambled eggs down center of each tortilla; roll up and place enchilada, seam side down, in a casserole dish. Repeat with each tortilla. Reheat remaining sauce to boiling. Pour evenly over enchiladas and sprinkle with cheese. Place under broiler, 4 inches from heat source, until cheese melts. Garnish with onion, jalapeños, and cilantro.

Orange Papaya Smoothie

Makes 4 servings

1 ripe papaya, peeled, seeded, and chopped
2 cups orange juice
1 cup plain yogurt

1 cup cracked ice
1 banana, mashed
1 teaspoon lime *or* lemon juice

Purée or process all ingredients until smooth. Serve in tall glasses.

Sunny Fruit Salad with
Ginger Dressing
Oranged Borscht
Breakfast Sandwiches

Sunny Fruit Salad

Makes 4 servings

2 small head Bibb *or*
  butterhead lettuce
½ avocado, sliced
1 nectarine, peeled and sliced
  into rounds

½ grapefruit, peeled and sliced
  into rounds
1 orange, peeled and sliced
  into rounds
  Ginger Dressing (below)

Separate lettuce into leaves. Arrange avocado, nectarine, grapefruit, and orange slices attractively over lettuce. Top with Ginger Dressing.
Note: Slices of peaches and papaya may be substituted for the nectarine, grapefruit, *or* orange.

Ginger Dressing
Makes 1 cup

1 cup plain yogurt
¼ cup orange juice

Sugar to taste
½ teaspoon minced fresh ginger

Stir all ingredients together. Let dressing stand at least 5 minutes before serving to blend flavors.

Variation
Omit minced ginger and add 2 teaspoons grated orange peel and a dash of ground cloves.

Oranged Borscht

Makes 4 servings

1 pound cooked beets, sliced
1 14½-ounce can low-sodium chicken broth
¼ cup coarsely chopped red onion
1 clove garlic

3 to 4 tablespoons orange juice
½ cup plain yogurt *or* Neufchatel cheese, softened
1 cucumber, peeled and diced
Orange slices

Process or blend first 5 ingredients until smooth. Stir in yogurt and cucumber. Chill and garnish with orange slices before serving.

Breakfast Sandwiches

Makes 4 servings

4 croissants, warmed and split in half
4 Open Omelets (page 11)

4 large mushrooms, thinly sliced
12 avocado slices

Layer all ingredients into croissants.

Variations

Ham and Cheese: Substitute omelets and mushrooms with 8 ounces sliced ham, 4 slices Swiss cheese, and 8 ounces sliced pineapple.

BLT: Substitute omelets and mushrooms with 8 cooked bacon strips, 4 lettuce leaves, and 4 tomato slices.

English Muffin Variation

2 English muffins, split
¼ cup butter *or* margarine
4 Open Omelets (page 11)

4 large mushrooms, thinly sliced
12 avocado slices

Toast muffins; spread with butter. Top with remaining ingredients. Serve open-faced.

Oranged Borscht, Breakfast Sandwiches, this page; Sunny Fruit Salad with Ginger Dressing, Page 5

Cantaloupe Fruit Boats with
Honey-Lemon Dressing
Spicy Scrambled Egg Pastries
Cornucopia Roll-Ups

Cantaloupe Fruit Boats with Honey-Lemon Dressing

Makes 4 servings

1 ripe cantaloupe *or* honey-dew melon
4 peaches, pitted and sliced
1 tablespoon lemon juice
2 teaspoons lime juice

2 plums, pitted and sliced
½ cup blueberries
½ cup raspberries
1 kiwi fruit, peeled and sliced
Honey-Lemon Dressing(below)

Cut melon into 4 wedges; discard seeds. Toss peach slices with lemon and lime juice. Mix together all fruits and fill each melon wedge. Top with Honey-Lemon Dressing.

Honey-Lemon Dressing

Makes 1 cup

1 cup plain yogurt
1 tablespoon honey
½ teaspoon dry mustard

1 teaspoon lemon juice
1 teaspoon lime juice

In a small bowl blend together all ingredients. Cover and chill until serving time.

Spicy Scrambled Egg Pastries

Makes 4 servings

1 tablespoon vegetable oil	1/3 cup salsa
1/3 cup julienne cut green pepper	1/4 cup finely chopped ham
1/3 cup julienne cut red pepper	10 eggs, beaten
2 to 3 tablespoons minced onion	8 puff pastry shells, baked according to package directions
1 clove garlic, minced	Salsa

In a medium skillet heat oil and sauté green and red peppers for 1 minute. Add onion and garlic and continue sautéing until onion becomes transparent and soft. Add salsa and ham; cook 5 minutes. Stir in eggs and scramble until firm but still moist. Serve eggs in puff pastry shells and garnish with extra salsa to taste.

Cornucopia Roll-Ups

Makes 4 servings

1 3-ounce package cream cheese	2 to 3 tablespoons milk
1 tablespoon curry powder	Freshly ground black pepper to taste
1/2 cup finely chopped pecans	12 turkey luncheon meat slices

Combine cheese, curry powder, and pecans. Stir in milk to moisten and season to taste. Spread over turkey slices and roll up into cornucopias.

Variations

Pineapple-Yogurt Cornucopias: Substitute 1/2 cup yogurt, 1/4 cup drained crushed pineapple, and 12 ham slices for the cream cheese, curry, and turkey.

Ham Rolls: Substitute ham slices and 2 to 3 tablespoons finely chopped ginger preserves for the turkey and curry powder.

Open Omelet Variations
Fresh Herb Scones
Apple Slaw

Open Omelet Variations

Makes 4 servings

4 eggs, separated
1/4 teaspoon salt
1/4 teaspoon cream of tartar

2 tablespoons water
1 to 2 teaspoon butter *or* margarine
1/2 to 1 cup topping of your choice

Preheat oven to 350°. Beat egg whites with salt and cream of tartar at high speed until stiff but not dry. Beat yolks with water at high speed until thick and lemon-colored, about 5 minutes. Fold yolks into whites.

Heat butter *or* margarine in 10-inch omelet pan over medium heat until just hot enough to sizzle a drop of water. Pour in omelet mixture and carefully smooth the surface. Cook until puffy and lightly browned on the bottom, about 5 minutes.

Bake in oven for about 10 minutes or until knife inserted in the center comes out clean. Cover surface with chosen topping. Cut in half or in wedges to serve. Garnish as desired.

Omelet Toppings

Light Lox: Drain and chop 2 slices smoked salmon. Combine with 4 ounces Neufchatel cheese until mixed. Spread on omelet. Sprinkle with lemon juice and chopped chives.

Garden Patch: Sauté or steam 1 cup sliced fresh vegetables of your choice. Garnish with lemon wedges.

Italian Sausage: Cook, drain, and crumble 2 Italian sausages. Combine with 1 large tomato, diced, and 2 tablespoons chopped fresh basil *or* 1 tablespoon dried basil. Ladle over omelet; sprinkle with grated Romano cheese.

Apple Slaw, Fresh Herb Scones, Page 12;
Open Omelet with Italian Sausage Topping, this page

Fresh Herb Scones

Makes 4 servings

2 cups all-purpose flour
½ cup whole wheat flour
1 to 2 teaspoons sugar
    substitute
2 teaspoons baking powder
1 teaspoon crushed rosemary
1 teaspoon baking soda

1 teaspoon salt
1 teaspoon thyme
1 teaspoon oregano
¼ cup butter or margarine
1 egg(reserve 1 tablespoon white)
½ cup plus 2 tablespoons
    buttermilk

Preheat oven to 400°. Combine or blend first 9 ingredients in bowl or food processor. Cut butter or margarine into small pieces and work into flour mixture with food processor or pastry blender until blended. In a separate bowl beat egg with buttermilk and stir into mixture. Turn dough out on a floured board and knead for 2 minutes. Shape into 2 thick circles, 5 inches in diameter. Cut each into quarters and place on lightly greased baking sheet with wedges about ½ inch apart. Brush with reserved egg white. Bake for 15 to 20 minutes or until nicely browned. Serve warm.

Apple Slaw

Makes 4 servings

⅓ cup plain yogurt
¼ cup sour cream
2 to 3 tablespoons minced chives
1 tablespoon lemon juice
1 teaspoon lime juice
1 tablespoon minced cilantro
    or parsley

1 teaspoon grated lemon rind
    Salt to taste
    Freshly ground pepper to taste
1 large red apple
1 cup grated peeled celery root
1 cup grated peeled jicama or turnip

In large bowl mix first 7 ingredients. Season to taste with salt and freshly ground pepper. Core apple but do not peel. Grate apple and add to yogurt mixture at once to keep apple from browning. Apple peel that does not pass through grater can be finely chopped. Blend in celery root and jicama. Let stand at room temperature for 30 minutes to blend flavors.

Oven Pancake
Sautéed Apples
Suggested Accompaniment:
Honeydew Melon with Lime Wedges

Oven Pancake

Makes 4 servings

6 eggs
1 cup milk
¼ cup butter *or* margarine, melted

1 cup all-purpose flour
¾ teaspoon salt
Melted butter *or* margarine
Sifted powdered sugar

In a blender combine eggs, milk, and melted butter *or* margarine. Cover and blend on low speed until mixed. Add flour and salt; cover and blend on medium speed until smooth. Pour into a well-greased 13 x 9 x 2-inch baking dish.

Bake at 450° for 20 to 22 minutes or until puffed and golden brown. Drizzle with melted butter and sprinkle with powdered sugar. Serve immediately.

Sautéed Apples

Makes 4 servings

4 medium apples, sliced
2 tablespoons butter *or* margarine

2 tablespoons granulated sugar
Dash Cinnamon

In a skillet cook and stir apples in hot butter *or* margarine over medium-high heat for 6 to 8 minutes or until tender. Stir in sugar and cinnamon. Serve hot.

Cheese-Filled Fig Tulips
Spinach Toss

Cheese-Filled Fig Tulips

Makes 4 servings

12 medium-large fresh figs
½ cup ricotta cheese
½ cup cream cheese
½ teaspoon lemon rind

½ teaspoon orange rind
½ teaspoon vanilla
3 to 4 tablespoons powdered sugar
12 unblanched whole almonds

Rinse figs and pat dry. Trim off stem. Cut each fig into 4 petals by cutting through fig from stem end to within ½ inch of the other end. (Cover and chill if made ahead.)

Process or blend remaining ingredients except almonds. Stand 2 to 3 figs upright on each plate. Gently open each fig and spoon in about 2 tablespoons of cheese mixture. Top each with an almond.

Spinach Toss

Makes 4 servings

½ cup salad oil
⅓ cup sugar
1 small onion, quartered
3 tablespoons vinegar
2 teaspoons prepared mustard

½ teaspoon celery seed
6 slices bacon, optional
6 cups torn spinach
1 cup sliced fresh mushrooms
2 hard-boiled eggs, chopped

To make dressing, in a blender container, combine oil, sugar, onion, vinegar, mustard, and celery seed. Cover and blend until smooth. Keep covered and chill. If desired, in a skillet fry bacon until crisp; drain and crumble. In a large salad bowl combine spinach, mushrooms, eggs, and bacon, if desired. Pour dressing over salad. Toss lightly.

Spinach Toss, this page

Menus with Chicken

Caviar and Olive Toast Rounds
Chicken in Red Pepper Butter
Mini Medley
Crabmeat Canapés

Mini Medley

Makes 4 servings

¼ **pound golden *or* red baby beets**
¼ **pound baby boiling onions**
¼ **pound baby carrots**
¼ **pound miniature zucchini**

Boiling salted water plus 2
tablespoons lemon juice
Minced parsley
Freshly grated Romano cheese

Trim all vegetables. Peel beets, onions, and carrots; steam over lemon-water for 10 minutes. Add zucchini and steam another 5 to 8 minutes. Toss with parsley and Romano.

Crabmeat Canapés

Makes 4 servings

1 **4-ounce can crabmeat, well**
drained
2 **tablespoon mayonnaise**
2 **tablespoons plain yogurt**
1 **tablespoon minced chives**

1 **tablespoon parsley**
1 **teaspoon lime juice**
1 **teaspoon Worcestershire sauce**
Freshly ground black pepper to taste
Melba toast rounds

Combine all ingredients except toast rounds; blend well. Spread on toast rounds and serve immediately.

Caviar and Olive Toast Rounds

Makes 4 servings

¼ cup caviar
10 to 12 stuffed green olives, finely chopped
2 to 3 tablespoons lemon juice

1 to 2 tablespoon minced red onion
Melba toast rounds
3 hard-boiled egg yolks, sieved

Mix first 4 ingredients. Spread on toast rounds and sprinkle with sieved yolks.

Chicken in Red Pepper Butter

Makes 4 servings

4 boneless skinless chicken breasts, halved
2 tablespoons butter *or* margarine

2 tablespoons vegetable oil
2 cloves garlic, minced
Red Pepper Butter (below)

Pound breasts to a thickness of ¼ inch. Heat butter *or* margarine, oil, and garlic in sauté pan. Sauté chicken breasts over medium-high heat, 3 to 5 minutes per side. Transfer to platter and keep warm in oven. Serve breasts with Red Pepper Butter.

Red Pepper Butter

Makes approximately 3 cups

2 tablespoons butter
2 medium shallots, minced
2½ medium red bell peppers, sliced
3 tablespoons raspberry vinegar *or* red wine vinegar

¼ cup fresh lemon juice
½ cup dry white wine *or* vermouth
1 cup unsalted butter, melted

Melt 2 tablespoons butter in medium saucepan; sauté shallots and peppers. Stew over low heat, stirring often, until shallots and peppers are softened, about 8 minutes. Add vinegar and cook on high heat until reduced by two-thirds. Add lemon juice and wine. Reduce by half. Transfer to food processor and purée until smooth, 1 to 1½ minutes. Add 1 cup melted butter in a thin stream while machine is running. Process 20 seconds longer. Just before serving, whisk sauce over low heat until hot to the touch. Do not simmer. *Note:* Red Pepper Butter can be prepared 3 hours ahead of time. Cover and store at room temperature until serving time.

Chicken Salad Croissants
Swiss Cheese Soup
Suggested Accompaniments:
Carrot Sticks and Apple Wedges

Chicken Salad Croissants

Makes 4 servings

2 cups diced cooked chicken
1 stalk celery, chopped
1 8½-ounce can crushed pineapple, drained
2 tablespoons sliced pimiento-stuffed olives

½ cup mayonnaise
Dash salt
Leaf lettuce
4 croissants, split
¼ cup chopped cashews

In a medium bowl combine chicken, celery, pineapple, and olives. Add mayonnaise and salt; toss together lightly. Cover and chill. To serve, place a lettuce leaf in each croissant. Spoon chicken salad over lettuce; sprinkle with cashews.

Swiss Cheese Soup

Makes 4 servings

3 tablespoons butter *or* margarine
¼ cup flour
1 teaspoon instant chicken bouillon granules

¼ teaspoon paprika
3½ cup milk
6 slices processed Swiss cheese
1 teaspoon snipped chives

Melt butter *or* margarine in medium saucepan. Stir in flour, bouillon granules, and paprika. Cook and stir over medium heat until bubbly. Add milk all at once. Cook and stir until thick and bubbly; cook and stir 1 minute more. Stir in cheese and chives. Stir over low heat until cheese melts.

Chicken Salad Croissants, this page

> Butter-Broiled Chicken
> Romaine and Artichoke Toss
> Suggested Accompaniment:
> Sautéed Mushrooms

Butter-Broiled Chicken

Makes 4 servings

6 tablespoons butter *or* margarine, melted
¼ teaspoon seasoning salt
¼ teaspoon dried oregano, crushed

Dash Garlic powder
Dash paprika
8 to 10 skinless chicken breasts

Preheat broiler. Combine butter *or* margarine, seasoning salt, oregano, garlic powder, and paprika. Place chicken on an unheated rack of a broiler pan. Brush lightly with butter mixture. Broil 5 to 6 inches from heat for 10 minutes, brushing occasionally with butter mixture. Turn; broil for 10 minutes more or until chicken is tender, brushing occasionally.

Romaine and Artichoke Toss

Makes 4 servings

1 6-ounce jar marinated artichoke hearts
¼ cup mayonnaise
2 tablespoons tarragon vinegar

1 tablespoon anchovy paste
1 teaspoon Dijon-style mustard
3 cups torn romaine

Drain artichoke hearts, reserving 2 tablespoons of the marinade. Cut up artichokes; set aside. To make dressing, combine mayonnaise, vinegar, anchovy paste, mustard, and reserved marinade. In a bowl combine romaine and artichokes; add dressing and toss.

Raspberry Glazed Chicken
Gourmet Onions
Suggested Accompaniment:
Steamed Broccoli

Raspberry Glazed Chicken

Makes 4 servings

1 2-pound whole roasting
   chicken
   Cooking oil
1/3 cup raspberry jelly
2 tablespoons lemon juice
1 tablespoon butter *or*
   margarine

1/4 teaspoon salt
   Dash ground cinnamon
1 tablespoon cold water
2 teaspoons cornstarch

Thoroughly rinse chicken; pat dry with paper towel. Place chicken, breast side up, on a rack in a shallow roasting pan. Rub skin with oil. Insert a meat thermometer in the center of the inside thigh muscle but not touching bone. Roast, uncovered, in a 375° oven for 1 1/4 to 1 1/2 hours or until thermometer registers 185°. In a small saucepan over low heat stir together jelly, lemon juice, butter *or* margarine, salt, and cinnamon until jelly melts. Combine water and cornstarch; stir into jelly mixture. Cook and stir over medium heat until thick and bubbly. Cook and stir 1 to 2 minutes more. Brush on chicken several times during the last 15 minutes of roasting.

Gourmet Onions

Makes 4 servings

6 medium onions, sliced
3 tablespoons butter *or*
   margarine

1/4 cup dry sherry
1/2 teaspoon sugar
2 tablespoons grated Parmesan cheese

In a 10-inch covered skillet cook onions in butter *or* margarine about 10 minutes until tender but not brown, stirring occasionally. Add sherry, sugar, 1/2 teaspoon salt, and dash pepper. Cook, uncovered, 2 to 3 minutes. Turn into a serving dish. Sprinkle with Parmesan cheese.

Smoked Salmon á la Russe
Poached Chicken and Vermicelli in Wine
Sherried Endive Salad
Brussels Sprouts and Creamed Carrots

Smoked Salmon á la Russe

Makes 4 servings

1 thin loaf French bread, sliced
  Sour cream
2 4-ounce packages smoked
  salmon, thinly sliced
4 ounces caviar

Butter lettuce cups
Capers
Tomato wedges
Lemon twists

Spread bread slices with sour cream. Shape salmon slices into coronets; spoon a little caviar into each coronet. Place coronets on bread slices and arrange on lettuce cups. Garnish with remaining ingredients.

Poached Chicken and Vermicelli in Wine

Makes 4 servings

1 teaspoon butter *or* margarine
1 teaspoon oil
½ pound mushrooms, sliced
4 boned chicken breasts,
  skinned and halved
¼ teaspoon salt

½ teaspoon tarragon
⅛ teaspoon pepper
2 tablespoons minced fresh parsley
¾ cup dry white wine
1 teaspoon arrowroot, optional
8 ounces vermicelli, cooked and drained

Melt butter *or* margarine and oil in a large skillet over medium-high heat. Sauté mushrooms and chicken until golden brown. Sprinkle with salt, tarragon, pepper, and parsley. Pour wine over chicken. Cover and simmer for 25 to 30 minutes. Remove chicken to serving platter. Deglaze skillet with a little water; thicken with one teaspoon arrowroot, if desired. Serve sauce with chicken and prepared vermicelli.

Poached Chicken and Vermicelli in Wine,
Smoked Salmon á la Russe, this page;
Sherried Endive Salad, Brussels Sprouts
and Creamed Carrots, page 24

Sherried Endive Salad

Makes 4 servings

12 medium *or* 8 large mush-
    rooms, trimmed
2 heads endive *or* escarole, torn
2 green onions, chopped

½ cup plain yogurt
1½ teaspoons Dijon-style mustard
1 to 2 tablespoons dry sherry

Arrange mushrooms on endive *or* escarole. Mix together remaining ingredients and spoon half of dressing over salad. Serve balance of dressing on the side.

Brussels Sprouts and Creamed Carrots

Makes 4 servings

1 pound Brussels sprouts
   Salt and freshly ground pepper

Creamed Carrots (below)

Trim off sprout ends and cut an "X" in the stem of each. Add sprouts to boiling water. Reduce heat; simmer, uncovered, until tender, 10 to 15 minutes. Drain; transfer to a serving platter and season with salt and ground pepper. Fit a pastry bag with a fluted tip. Pipe a rosette of Creamed Carrots on each Brussels sprout. Pipe remaining Creamed Carrots around edge of platter.

Creamed Carrots
Makes 4 servings

3 carrots, sliced diagonally
4 ounces Neufchatel cheese
2 tablespoons plain yogurt

¼ teaspoon tarragon
   Skim milk

Steam carrots until tender, 5 to 8 minutes. Combine with remaining ingredients and purée until smooth. Thin with milk, if necessary. Serve with Brussels sprouts as directed.

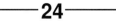

Honey Dip with Fruit
Chicken Jambalaya
Broiled Sourdough Slices
Tomato-Carrot Salad

Honey Dip with Fruit

Makes 1 cup

1 tablespoon honey
½ cup Neufchatel *or* ricotta cheese
½ cup plain yogurt

Grated peel of ½ lime *or* ½ lemon
Grated peel of ½ orange
1 tablespoon jam *or* preserves
Choice of fruits

Combine all ingredients; mix well. Serve as a dip with your favorite fruits prepared in bite-size pieces.

Tomato-Carrot Salad

Makes 4 servings

4 lettuce leaves
4 large tomatoes, cut into wedges
2 large carrots, grated
⅔ cup peanut oil
Juice and grated rind of one orange

1 tablespoon red wine vinegar
1 teaspoon Dijon-style mustard
1 teaspoon sugar
Salt and freshly ground black pepper
Orange wedges

Line 4 bowls with lettuce leaves and top with tomatoes and carrots. Combine remaining ingredients. Pour dressing over each salad just before serving and serve the balance on the side. Garnish with orange wedges.

Chicken Jambalaya

Makes 4 servings

2 to 3 cloves garlic, minced
½ cup chopped red onion
1 stalk celery, sliced
2 hot chorizos, casings removed and broken up
2 tablespoons olive oil *or* vegetable oil
1 cup chicken broth
1 cup white wine

1 cup long-grain white rice
1 16-ounce can stewed tomatoes, chopped
1 teaspoon thyme *or* oregano leaves
½ teaspoon turmeric
¼ teaspoon red pepper
½ 20-ounce package frozen peas
1 pound medium-size raw shrimp, in shells *or* frozen shrimp

Sauté first 4 ingredients 3 to 5 minutes in hot oil. Add next 7 ingredients. Bring to a boil. Reduce heat; cover and simmer 15 minutes. Add peas and shrimp. Cover and cook 5 minutes. Toss with a fork to fluff rice and distribute shrimp.
Note: 8 fresh mussels or clams may be substituted for ½ pound of shrimp.

Broiled Sourdough Slices

Makes 4 servings

½ loaf sourdough French bread
½ cup butter *or* margarine, softened
2 to 3 cloves garlic, minced

¼ cup minced fresh parsley
¼ cup freshly grated Romano *or* Parmesan cheese

Preheat broiler. Slice French bread. Blend remaining ingredients and spread evenly over bread slices. Broil until golden and bubbly.

Chicken Jambalaya, Broiled Sourdough Slices, this page; Fruit with Honey Dip, Tomato-Carrot Salad, page 25

Vegetable Fromage
Gingered Chicken with Apples
Rosemary Macaroni
Fruited Watercress Salad

Vegetable Fromage

Makes 4 servings

2 8-ounce packages cream
  cheese
¼ cup plain yogurt
¼ cup shredded carrot
¼ cup finely chopped radish

¼ cup finely chopped red pepper
¼ cup finely chopped green pepper
¼ cup finely sliced green onion *or*
  cilantro
  Whole-grain breadsticks

Process cream cheese, yogurt, carrot, radish, red pepper, green pepper, and green onion or blend well with a wooden spoon. Use immediately or refrigerate, covered, up to 2 days. Bring to room temperature before serving with whole-grain breadsticks.

Rosemary Macaroni

Makes 4 servings

2 quarts water
½ teaspoon salt
8 ounces elbow macaroni (whole
  wheat, yellow, and/or green)

1 tablespoon oil
1 teaspoon lemon juice
  Chopped fresh rosemary *or* chives

Bring water and salt to a boil. Add macaroni, oil, and lemon juice and cook until tender but firm. Add rosemary and toss before serving.

Gingered Chicken with Apples

Makes 4 servings

1 tablespoon safflower oil *or* vegetable oil
2½ pounds chicken, cut into pieces
¼ cup Cognac
½ cup evaporated skim milk
½ cup non-fat milk

1 tablespoon chopped gingerroot *or* ½ teaspoon ground ginger
½ teaspoon nutmeg
1½ cups thinly sliced tart apples
1 teaspoon arrowroot, optional
Toasted slivered almonds
Chopped candied ginger

Heat oil in a large skillet. Add chicken, skin side down; brown well on all sides. Remove and set aside. Deglaze pan with Cognac. Flambé if desired. Return browned chicken to skillet.

To make cream sauce, combine next 5 ingredients. Add to skillet and gently simmer 20 to 30 minutes. Remove chicken to serving platter. Add apples to skillet. Cook until just tender, 1 to 2 minutes. Thicken with arrowroot, if desired. Serve apples and sauce over chicken. Garnish with almonds and candied ginger.

Fruited Watercress Salad

Makes 4 servings

2 oranges, peeled and sliced
2 kiwi fruit, peeled and sliced
1 grapefruit, peeled and sliced
2 bunches watercress, tough stems removed

1 head butter lettuce, cleaned and separated into leaves
Lemon *or* lime juice
Vegetable oil

Arrange fruit on a bed of watercress and butter lettuce. Sprinkle with juice and oil to taste.

Menus with Pork

Carrots Purée in Zucchini Boats
Mustard-Broiled Pork Chops
Pasta with Garlic
Grilled Cheese and Walnut Salad
with Mango Dressing

Carrots Purée in Zucchini Boats

Makes 4 servings

1 tablespoon butter *or* margarine
1 pound carrots, thinly sliced
3 tablespoons water
½ cup evaporated milk

1 to 2 tablespoons dry sherry
¼ teaspoon nutmeg
¼ teaspoon cinnamon
4 medium zucchini, baked until soft

Melt butter *or* margarine in large skillet; add carrots and water. Steam, covered, until tender, 5 to 8 minutes. In a blender combine carrots with next 4 ingredients; blend until smooth. Split zucchini lengthwise and scoop out seeds. Spoon carrot purée into each zucchini shell, or pipe, using a pastry bag fitted with a rosette tip.

Mustard-Broiled Pork Chops

Makes 4 servings

¼ cup Dijon-style mustard
4 pork loin chops, ¾ inch thick, trimmed

Freshly ground pepper to taste

Preheat broiler. Spread half of the mustard evenly over chops. Broil 6 inches away from heat source for 8 to 10 minutes. Turn chops; spread with remaining mustard. Grind pepper over chops. Broil another 10 minutes.

Mustard-Broiled Pork Chops, Carrots Purée in Zucchini Boats, this page; Pasta with Garlic, Grilled Cheese and Walnut Salad with Mango Dressing, page 32

—————31—————

Pasta with Garlic

Makes 4 servings

2 cups chicken broth
2 cups water
½ pound fresh pasta
1 tablespoon butter *or* margarine
2 cloves garlic, minced

¼ cup minced fresh parsley
1 teaspoon basil, marjoram, oregano, *or* thyme
Freshly grated Parmesan, Romano, *or* Sapsago cheese

Bring broth and water to a boil in a large pot. Add pasta and cook until tender but still firm, 4 to 6 minutes. Drain and transfer to a heated platter. Melt butter *or* margarine in a small saucepan and stir in garlic, parsley, and herbs. Heat gently. Pour parsley mixture over noodles and toss to coat well. Garnish with grated cheese.

Grilled Cheese and Walnut Salad with Mango Dressing

Makes 4 servings

1 head radicchio
1 head butter lettuce
1 head Arugula
4 to 6 ounces mild herbed goat cheese
½ cup walnut *or* hazelnut oil *or* vegetable oil

1 tablespoon mango chutney
1 tablespoon plain yogurt
2 teaspoons red wine vinegar
1 cup coarsely chopped walnuts

Discard any outer leaves, then wash and pat dry all greens. Refrigerate. Slice cheese into four chunks. Grill or broil briefly and set aside. Process or blend next 4 ingredients for dressing. Arrange lettuce leaves on a platter. Form a ring of Arugula over lettuce. Place cheese in center. Sprinkle with walnuts and drizzle on dressing.

Pork Chops with Brown Rice
Broiled Tomatoes
Suggested Accompaniment:
Mixed Green Salad
with Blue Cheese Dressing

Pork Chops with Brown Rice

Makes 4 servings

4 pork chops, about 1 pound
1 tablespoon cooking oil
1 4⅝-ounce package quick-cooking brown and wild rice mix with mushrooms

1⅓ cup water
1 stalk celery, sliced
½ cup sour cream

In a skillet brown chops in hot oil over medium heat. Remove chops from the skillet; discard drippings. In the same skillet combine rice mix, water, and celery; place chops over rice mixture. Bring to a boil. Reduce heat and simmer, covered, for 30 minutes. Remove chops from the skillet; keep warm. Stir sour cream into rice mixture; heat through but do not boil. Serve with chops.

Broiled Tomatoes

Makes 4 servings

2 large ripe tomatoes
¾ cup soft bread crumbs
¼ cup grated Parmesan cheese

2 tablespoons butter *or* margarine, melted
¼ teaspoon dried crushed basil

Preheat broiler. Halve each tomato crosswise. Place cut side up in a shallow baking pan. Combine bread crumbs, Pamesan cheese, butter *or* margarine, and basil; sprinkle over tomatoes. Broil 3 to 4 inches from the heat source for about 4 minutes or until lightly browned.

Menus with Fish and Shellfish

Stuffed Pea Pods
Broiled Swordfish
Lemon-Dill Rice
Carrots in Lime Butter
Italian Tomato Cucumber Salad

Stuffed Pea Pods

Makes 4 servings

25 snow peas
4 ounces goat cheese
   (Montrachet *or* Lezay)
¼ cup plain yogurt

1 teaspoon any flavored mustard
½ cup finely chopped Hot and
   Spicy Pecans (below)

Cut stem ends of snow peas and pull down straight edge to remove any string. Blanch in boiling water for 30 seconds. Plunge peas into ice water. Using a sharp paring knife, slit open each pod along straight side. In bowl combine cheese, yogurt, mustard, and ¼ cup pecans. Pipe or stuff each pod with goat cheese mixture. Dip stuffing side of each pod into remaining chopped nuts to garnish.

Hot and Spicy Pecans

Makes 2 cups

2 cups pecan halves
Butter *or* margarine, melted
Cayenne
Cumin

Paprika
Cloves
Onion salt *or* chili powder

Roast pecans in 300° oven for 20 minutes. Sprinkle with remaining ingredients to taste. Use for Stuffed Pea Pods as directed; serve balance of pecans on the side.

—— **34** ——

Carrots in Lime Butter, Lemon-Dill Rice, page 36; Broiled Swordfish, Italian Tomato Cucumber Salad, page 37

Lemon-Dill Rice

Makes 4 servings

1 tablespoon safflower oil
  or vegetable oil
1 cup long-grain brown *or*
  white rice
1 cup finely chopped red onion
1 stalk finely chopped celery
1 large garlic clove, minced
1 13-ounce can chicken broth

⅓ cup water
1 to 2 tablespoons lemon juice
¼ cup minced fresh dill *or*
  1 tablespoon dried dill
Freshly ground pepper
Fresh dill sprigs
Lemon slices

Heat safflower oil over medium-high heat. Add rice, onion, celery, and garlic; sauté about 5 minutes. Add broth, water, and lemon juice. Bring to a boil; reduce heat and simmer, covered, 20 to 30 minutes. Stir in minced dill and pepper. Remove from heat. Cover and let stand 10 minutes. Garnish with dill sprigs and lemon slices.

Carrots in Lime Butter

Makes 4 servings

1 pound carrots
4½ cups water
2 tablespoons sugar

1 to 2 tablespoons unsalted butter
2 tablespoons fresh lime juice

Cut carrots diagonally into ¼-inch thick slices. In medium saucepan bring carrots and 4 cups cold water to a full boil. Boil for 3 to 5 minutes; drain. Return carrots to saucepan. Add ½ cup water and sugar. Bring to a boil over medium heat; cook until carrots are just tender and the liquid is reduced to 1 or 2 tablespoons, about 7 minutes. Stir in butter and lime juice.

Italian Tomato Cucumber Salad

Makes 4 servings

5 or 6 Italian-style plum tomatoes
   or 3 large ripe tomatoes
1 stalk celery, thinly sliced
1 cucumber, sliced
3 or 4 red onions, sliced
1 clove garlic, halved

Black peppercorn
Chopped fresh oregano
Minced fresh basil
2 tablespoons olive oil or
   vegetable oil
2 tablespoons red wine vinegar

Cut tomatoes into wedges and combine with celery, cucumber, and onion. Rub a glass serving bowl with cut side of garlic; add vegetables. Grind pepper over all and season generously with oregano and basil. Drizzle oil and vinegar evenly over salad; toss gently. Serve at room temperature.

Broiled Swordfish

Makes 4 servings

Freshly ground pepper
4 1¾-pound swordfish or hali-
   but steaks, cut 1 inch thick
1 tablespoon butter
1 large red pepper, cut into
   julienne strips
1 large green pepper, cut into
   julienne strips

4 tablespoons lemon juice
¼ cup grated Parmesan cheese
2 tablespoons chopped fresh basil,
   optional
Lemon wedges

Preheat broiler to high. Grind pepper generously over swordfish. Heat butter over medium-high heat; add peppers and sauté until tender and well browned, about 10 minutes. Set aside. Broil swordfish 4 to 5 inches from heat source for 3 minutes. Sprinkle 2 tablespoons of lemon juice evenly over steaks. Turn fish, sprinkle remaining juice and broil for 5 minutes more or until fish flakes easily when tested with a fork. Spread peppers evenly over swordfish; sprinkle with Parmesan cheese and basil. Garnish with lemon wedges.

Cheese and Apple Wafers
Mexican Snapper
Steamed New Potatoes and Sesame Carrots
Green Salad with Mexican Dressing

Cheese and Apple Wafers

Makes 4 servings

1 cup flour	Minced chives, cilantro, *or* parsley
1¼ cup grated Cheddar cheese	Poppy, caraway, *or* sesame seeds
¼ pound butter *or* margarine	Apple *or* pear wedges
1 teaspoon Worcestershire sauce	

Combine flour and cheese; cut in butter *or* margarine. Add sauce and blend well. Roll dough into long strips about ³/₄ inch in diameter. Freeze 15 minutes. Slice into thin wafers. Bake at 475° for 10 minutes on greased cookie sheet. Sprinkle wafers with different combinations of minced chives, cilantro, *or* parsley; poppy, caraway, *or* sesame seeds. Serve with apple wedges.

Mexican Snapper

Makes 4 servings

1½ pounds red snapper or cod fillets	¼ cup butter *or* margarine
	Lime juice
½ cup chopped cilantro *or* parsley	Salt and pepper to taste
½ cup finely chopped toasted almonds	Diced avocados

Place fish fillets in a baking dish. Sprinkle with cilantro and almonds. Melt butter *or* margarine in saucepan; add lime juice and season to taste. Pour over fish. Cover and bake in a 350° oven for 30 minutes. Sprinkle with diced avocados and serve.

Mexican Snapper, Cod Variation, this page; Steamed New Potatoes and Sesame Carrots, Green Salad with Mexican Dressing, page 40

Steamed New Potatoes and Sesame Carrots

Makes 4 servings

10 to 12 small new potatoes
10 to 12 medium carrots
 1 teaspoon butter *or* margarine
 2 tablespoons sesame seeds
 2 tablespoons butter *or* margarine

1 tablespoon honey
1 tablespoon grated orange rind
1 teaspoon grated gingerroot
Minced Parsley

Scrub potatoes but do not peel. Slice thinly and place in steamer. Peel and cut carrots into 3-inch sticks. Place in steamer above potatoes. Steam 15 minutes until tender. Melt 1 tablespoon butter *or* margarine in a medium skillet; add sesame seeds and toast until golden. Add the 2 tablespoons butter *or* margarine, honey, orange rind, and gingerroot; blend well. Remove carrots from steamer; toss in sesame glaze. Remove potatoes and sprinkle with parsley.

Green Salad with Mexican Dressing

Makes 4 servings

6 large radishes, sliced
1 large tomato, cut in wedges
4 to 6 large mushrooms, sliced
1 avocado, sliced
3 fresh peaches, sliced
¼ head iceberg lettuce, torn into
   bite-size pieces

¼ head romaine lettuce, torn into
   bite-size pieces
Mexican Dressing (below)
Shredded sharp Cheddar cheese

Arrange vegetables and fruit over lettuce in a large bowl. Add Mexican Dressing; toss and garnish with cheese. Serve immediately.

Mexican Dressing
Makes 1¼ cups

½ cup mild *or* hot taco sauce
¼ cup red wine vinegar
¼ cup olive oil
1 tablespoon minced parsley

1 tablespoon diced green chilies
1 teaspoon minced cilantro
1 teaspoon minced fresh oregano
   or ¼ teaspoon dried oregano

Combine all ingredients; mix thoroughly. Serve as directed.

> Stir-Fry Pasta Primavera
> Seafood Foil

Stir-Fry Pasta Primavera

Makes 4 servings

½ cup unsalted butter
1 medium onion, minced
2 large cloves garlic, minced
1 pound asparagus, cut diagonally in ¼-inch slices, tips intact
½ pound cauliflower, broken up
½ pound mushrooms, sliced
1 zucchini, cut in ¼-inch slices
1 small carrot, halved lengthwise and cut in ⅛-inch slices

½ cup chicken broth
¼ cup dry white wine
1 teaspoon dried basil leaves
½ teaspoon oregano leaves
1 cup frozen early peas, thawed
5 green onions, chopped
2 tablespoons minced parsley
Salt and pepper to taste
1 pound linguine, cooked and drained
½ cup grated Parmesan cheese

Heat wok or large, deep skillet over medium-high heat. Add butter, onion, and garlic; stir-fry until onion is tender, about 2 minutes. Stir in asparagus, cauliflower, mushrooms, zucchini, and carrot; stir-fry 2 minutes. Increase heat to high. Add broth, wine, basil, and oregano. Bring to a boil; boil until liquid is slightly reduced, about 3 minutes. Add peas and green onions; heat through, stirring gently, for 1 minute. Add parsley, salt, and pepper. Add pasta and cheese; toss until cheese is evenly distributed and pasta is heated through.

Seafood Foil

Makes 4 servings

4 1- to 1½-pound fish fillets (snapper, cod, or orange roughy)
½ cup thick salsa

8 large shrimp
Cilantro sprigs or parsley
1 lime, cut into wedges

Cut foil into 8 heart-shaped pieces 1 inch longer than fillets. Place a fillet on each heart; top with 2 tablespoons salsa, 2 shrimp, and 2 sprigs of cilantro. Cover with another foil heart; seal edges. Bake at 400° for 10 to 12 minutes. Transfer to dinner plates. Cut a large "X" in each foil packet; turn back foil to expose fish. Garnish with lime wedges and serve steaming hot.

Broiled Shrimp Kebabs
Pasta and Pea Pods

Broiled Shrimp Kebabs

Makes 4 servings

1 pound fresh large shrimp
   in shells
¼ cup safflower oil
4 lemon slices
4 whole allspice

3 cloves garlic, minced
1 teaspoon crushed dried tarragon
1 teaspoon crushed dried oregano
   Bay leaves, optional

Peel and devein shrimp, leaving tail intact. In a shallow dish combine oil, lemon, allspice, garlic, tarragon, and oregano. Add shrimp. Cover and marinate for 1 hour at room temperature, stirring occasionally. Preheat broiler. Drain shrimp, reserving marinade; discard lemon and allspice. Thread shrimp on short skewers alternately with bay leaves, if desired. Place on unheated rack of broiler pan. Broil 4 inches from heat source for 3 to 4 minutes or until shrimp turn pink. Turn and brush occasionally with reserved marinade.

Pasta and Pea Pods

Makes 4 servings

8 ounces mostaccioli
1 6-ounce package frozen pea
   pods
½ cup butter *or* margarine

Salt and pepper to taste
¼ cup grated Romano cheese
   Julienned carrots, optional

Cook mostaccioli and pea pods according to package directions; drain and keep warm. In a skillet melt butter *or* margarine over medium heat until golden brown. Remove from heat; add mostaccioli and pea pods. Toss together. Season to taste with salt and pepper. Transfer to a serving bowl; sprinkle with Romano cheese. Garnish with julienned carrots, if desired.

> Oven-Fried Fish
> Crab-Stuffed Mushrooms
> Suggested Accompaniment:
> Coleslaw

Oven-Fried Fish

Makes 4 servings

1 pound fresh fish fillets, thawed, cut ½-inch thick
1 beaten egg
2 tablespoons milk
¼ cup fine dry seasoned bread crumbs

2 tablespoons yellow cornmeal
2 tablespoons all-purpose flour
¼ teaspoon seasoned salt
6 tablespoons butter *or* margarine, melted
Lemon wedges

Rinse fish and pat dry. In a shallow dish combine egg and milk. In a second shallow dish combine crumbs, cornmeal, flour, and salt. Dip fish in egg mixture, then in crumb mixture. Place in a shallow baking pan. Drizzle fish with melted butter. Bake at 500° for 4 to 6 minutes or until fish flakes easily when tested with a fork. Serve with lemon wedges.

Crab-Stuffed Mushrooms

Makes 4 servings

3 tablespoons butter *or* margarine
12 large mushroom caps
2 cloves garlic, minced
½ cup monterey Jack *or* mozzarella cheese, shredded

1 6-ounce can flaked crabmeat
2 tablespoons red *or* white wine
1 to 2 teaspoons Worcestershire sauce
2 tablespoons fine dry bread crumbs
Freshly ground pepper
Shredded Monterey Jack cheese

Melt 1 tablespoon butter *or* margarine in sauté pan. Sauté mushroom caps, coating well with butter. Combine remaining butter *or* margarine and next 6 ingredients until blended. Place mushrooms on rimmed baking sheet. Evenly mound filling into each mushroom cavity, pressing lightly. Sprinkle with pepper and cheese. Broil about 6 inches from heat source 5 to 8 minutes. Serve immediately.

Steamed Vegetables
Chilled Fruit Soup
Crudités with Garlic Dip
Champagned Fish with Parsley Butter

Steamed Vegetables

Makes 4 servings

2 medium carrots, thinly sliced	1 cup cauliflower florets
¼ cup green beans, cut into thirds	1 tablespoon fresh lemon juice
	1 teaspoon grated lemon peel

Steam vegetables over boiling water until tender-crisp, about 8 minutes. Toss in a serving bowl with lemon juice and peel.

Chilled Fruit Soup

Makes 4 servings

5 large ripe bananas, peeled and quartered *or* 1 bag frozen peaches *or* nectarines, thawed	2 tablespoons orange juice concentrate, thawed
2 tablespoons sugar	1 tablespoon lemon juice
½ cup Neufchatel cheese	2 to 3 tablespoons sweet *or* cream sherry
¼ cup plain yogurt	Kiwi fruit slices
	Fresh mint sprigs

In a blender or food processor blend all ingredients, except kiwi and mint, until smooth. Taste and add additional lemon or sherry as desired. Pour into a serving bowl; cover and chill. Garnish with kiwi fruit slices and fresh mint sprigs.

Crudités with Garlic Dip

Makes 4 servings

4 medium cloves garlic	½ teaspoon cold water
2 large egg yolks, at room temperature	1 cup cauliflower florets, steamed
⅛ teaspoon salt	1 cup broccoli florets, steamed
¼ teaspoon Dijon-style mustard	4 green onions, trimmed
¾ cup olive oil	½ cup fresh mushrooms
1 teaspoon lemon juice	4 carrots, cut into 3-inch sticks
	4 stalks celery, cut into 3-inch sticks

Crush garlic and reduce to a paste; place in a blender or food processor. Add egg yolks, salt, and mustard; blend briefly. Gradually stir in half the oil. Add lemon and water; add the remaining oil; blend slowly and steadily. Transfer to a glass serving bowl; cover and refrigerate. To serve, place dip in the center of a large platter and arrange vegetables around it.

Champagned Fish with Parsley Butter

Makes 4 servings

Freshly ground pepper	½ cup champagne
4 1¼-pound fish steaks, cut 1 inch thick (halibut, swordfish, *or* salmon)	Parsley Butter (below)

Grind pepper generously over steaks. Pour champagne evenly over fish. Broil 4 inches from heat source for 3 to 5 minutes. Turn. Broil 4 minutes more or until fish flakes easily when tested with a fork. Top with a spoonful of Parsley Butter.

Parsley Butter

Makes ¾ cup

½ cup butter, at room temperature	½ cup chopped fresh parsley
¼ cup grated Parmesan cheese	1 to 2 cloves garlic, minced

Combine all ingredients; blend well. Serve as directed.

Chicken Puffs
Trout Meuniere
Asparagus with Blender Bearnaise
Herbed Squash and Mushrooms
Spinach Salad with
Lemon-Lime Vinaigrette

Chicken Puffs

Makes 1 dozen pastries

½ package (10 ounces) puff
  pastry sheets
1 tablespoon butter
1 small red onion, minced
2 teaspoons curry
1 teaspoon chopped chutney

1 tablespoon chopped walnuts
  or almonds
1 tablespoon shredded coconut
½ cup half-and-half
1 cup chopped cooked chicken

Roll out one sheet puff pastry. Cut out 1½-inch rounds with fluted cookie cutter. Bake in oven according to package directions. Melt butter in a large saucepan. Sauté onion until golden. Stir in curry, chutney, nuts, and coconut; cook 3 to 5 minutes. Add half-and-half and bring to a boil. Simmer 5 minutes. Add chicken and blend well. Serve warm or cold on puff pastry shells.

Herbed Squash and Mushrooms

Makes 4 servings

1 pound (4 small) crookneck *or*
  zucchini squash, quartered
½ pound mushrooms, halved

¼ cup chicken broth
½ teaspoon dried basil or tarragon
  Salt and pepper to taste

Place all ingredients in a skillet; cover and simmer until tender-crisp, 6 to 8 minutes.

Asparagus with Blender Bearnaise

Makes 4 servings

2 pounds asparagus	1 to 2 tablespoons butter
Boiling salted water	Blender Bernaise(below)

Wash asparagus and cut or snap off tough ends. In a wide frying pan with a little boiling water, lay spears parallel no more than three layers deep. Cook, uncovered, over high heat until stems are just tender when pierced with a fork, 6 to 8 minutes. Drain. Top with butter and serve with Blender Bearnaise.

Note: For lighter appetites, omit Blender Bearnaise and serve asparagus with Meuniere Sauce from Trout recipe.

Blender Bearnaise

Makes 1 cup

¼ cup wine vinegar	6 black peppercorns
¼ cup vermouth *or* white wine	6 parsley sprigs
1 shallot *or* green onion, minced	1 cup butter
1 teaspoon dried tarragon leaves	3 egg yolks
1 bay leaf	

In a small saucepan bring first 7 ingredients to a boil; reduce to 3 tablespoons. Melt butter in a separate saucepan. In blender whirl yolks until just blended. Add reduced wine mixture and blend briefly. Add melted butter, a droplet at a time, blending continuously on high speed. As mixture thickens, increase butter to a thin stream. Keep sauce warm by placing blender container in a pan of lukewarm water, if desired.

Note: For a faster Hollandaise version, simply omit first 7 ingredients and the first step. Proceed as directed. Makes ½ cup.

Curry Bearnaise Variation

Makes 1 cup

1 tablespoon vegetable oil	1 tablespoon curry powder
½ small onion, chopped	¾ cup plain yogurt

Heat oil in skillet; sauté onion until tender. Stir in curry; cook 3 to 4 minutes, stirring constantly. Transfer to a blender or food processor. Add yogurt; blend until smooth.

Trout Meuniere

Makes 4 servings

4 medium trout
Lemon juice
Freshly ground black pepper
2 tablespoons butter
2 tablespoons oil

¼ cup butter
¼ cup lemon juice *or* white wine
¼ cup minced fresh parsley
  Sliced kiwi, avocado, *or* mango

Rub trout with lemon juice and pepper. Warm platter for fish in 200° oven. Heat butter and oil in a large frying pan over medium-high heat. Add trout and sauté until lightly browned on one side; when edges become opaque and curl slightly, 3 to 5 minutes, turn. Heat until fish flakes easily when tested with a fork in the thickest portion. Remove fish to warm platter.

Wipe out pan and melt butter. Add lemon juice and parsley all at once. Swirl and pour sauce over trout. Garnish with kiwi slices.

Spinach Salad with Lemon-Lime Vinaigrette

Makes 4 servings

1 bunch spinach, stems removed
3 green onions, sliced
½ cup sliced radishes

1 cup bean sprouts, optional
6 to 8 cherry tomatoes, halved
  Lemon-Lime Vinaigrette (below)

Tear spinach into bite-size pieces. Arrange other vegetables in groups on top of spinach. Serve with Lemon-Lime Vinaigrette.

Lemon-Lime Vinaigrette
Makes 1 cup

¼ cup safflower oil
2 tablespoons lemon juice

2 tablespoons lime juice
2 tablespoons minced parsley

Combine all ingredients; mix well.

Trout Meuniere, Spinach Salad with Lemon-Lime Vinaigrette, this page; Herbed Squash and Mushrooms, page 48; Asparagus with Blender Bearnaise, page 49

Parmesan Pinwheels
Broiled Salmon with Linguine
and Watercress Sauce
Sliced Beefsteak Tomatoes

Sliced Beefsteak Tomatoes

Makes 4 servings

3 large beefsteak tomatoes
⅓ cup olive oil
¼ cup lemon juice
1 tablespoon chopped fresh basil
   or ½ teaspoon dried basil

1 tablespoon freshly chopped rosemary
   or ½ teaspoon dried rosemary

Slice tomatoes. Whisk together remaining ingredients; pour over tomatoes. Let stand at room temperature until serving.

Broiled Salmon with Linguine and Watercress Sauce

Makes 4 servings

4 salmon steaks, ¾ inch thick
1 tablespoon chopped fresh mar-joram *or* 1 teaspoon dried marjoram

Salt and pepper to taste
Watercress Sauce(next page)
4 ounces thin linguine, cooked and well drained

Sprinkle both sides of fish with marjoram and salt and pepper to taste. On an oiled rack 4 inches from heat source broil steaks until first side is lightly browned, 5 to 8 minutes. Turn and broil 5 to 8 minutes more, until fish flakes easily when tested with a fork. Combine ¾ cup of Watercress Sauce with prepared linguine. Serve balance of the Watercress Sauce over the salmon steaks.

Watercress Sauce

Makes 2 cups

1 cup tightly packed parsley
1 cup watercress leaves
6 large Boston lettuce leaves,
  centers removed
3 large shallots, quartered

1 small onion, cut into 1-inch chunks
3 tablespoons olive oil
1 tablespoon wine vinegar
1/3 cup unsalted tomato juice

Fit food processor with steel blade. Combine parsley, watercress, lettuce, shallots, and onions in work bowl; process with 3 on/off turns. Scrape down sides of bowl. Pour olive oil over mixture in a circular motion. Sprinkle with vinegar. Purée for 5 seconds. While machine is running, pour tomato juice through feed tube until well blended. Serve with salmon and linguine as directed.

Parmesan Pinwheels

Makes 4 servings

1 cup butter *or* margarine
1 cup flour
1/2 cup shredded sharp Meunster
  or sharp Brick cheese
1/2 cup sour cream
2/3 cup freshly grated Parmesan *or*
  Romano cheese

1/2 teaspoon cayenne pepper
1/2 teaspoon paprika
1/4 teaspoon salt
1/4 teaspoon Tabasco sauce
Fresh-cut vegetables *or* fruit, optional

Using a pastry blender, cut together butter *or* margarine and flour. Blend in Meunster cheese and sour cream. Divide dough into 4 parts; wrap and chill for 15 minutes. Combine Parmesan, pepper, paprika, salt, and Tabasco sauce; set aside. On a floured surface roll one part of pastry into a 12 x 6-inch rectangle. Sprinkle with 2 tablespoons of the Parmesan mixture. Fold in 6-inch sides to meet in center, forming a square. Sprinkle with 1 tablespoon of the Parmesan mixture. Fold lengthwise again. On folded edge make 1/4-inch cuts, 1 inch apart. Bring ends together, forming a wheel, and place on ungreased baking sheet. Repeat with remaining pastry sections. Bake 10 to 15 minutes at 450° or until golden brown. Serve with vegetables *or* fruit, if desired.

Menus with Lamb and Veal

Lamb Chops Persillade
Tomato Shells with Vegetable Purée
Suggested Accompaniment:
Long-Grain and Wild Rice with Mushrooms

Lamb Chops Persillade

Makes 4 servings

4 lamb loin chops, 1 inch thick
2 cloves garlic, minced and stirred to paste
1 tablespoon butter
3 tablespoons minced shallots

⅓ cup fine bread crumbs
⅓ cup minced fresh parsley
1 teaspoon tarragon, basil, *or* thyme
Freshly ground pepper
Grated Parmesan cheese

Line broiler pan with foil to collect drippings. Rub chops with garlic paste. Broil 4 inches from heat source for 6 to 8 minutes on each side. Melt butter in a saucepan; sauté shallots and bread crumbs until golden brown. Remove from heat. Stir in parsley, herbs, and drippings from lamb chops. Add pepper and cheese to taste. Spread over one side of chops before serving.

Tomato Shells with Vegetable Purée

Makes 4 servings

1 pound broccoli, chopped
2 chayotes, peeled and sliced
2 large tomatoes, room temperature
¼ cup Neufchatel cheese

¼ cup ricotta cheese
Dash nutmeg *or* cayenne
Freshly ground pepper
Grated Romano cheese

Steam broccoli and chayote until tender, 12 minutes. Make deep zigzag cuts around the tomatoes; twist and pull gently apart. Scoop out pulp and seeds; set shells on a warm platter. In a blender process green vegetables, Neufchatel, ricotta, nutmeg, and pepper until smooth. Pour into tomato shells. Sprinkle with cheese. Broil until cheese is golden and tomato is hot.

Lamb Chops Persillade, Tomato Shells
with Vegetable Purée, this page

Veal and Artichoke Sauté
Fresh Herbed Pasta
Sautéed Medley
Chilled Watercress Soup

Veal and Artichoke Sauté

Makes 4 servings

1 pound veal *or* turkey cutlets,
  cut to finger lengths
  Flour
  Salt and pepper
½ teaspoon sage
2 tablespoons butter *or* margarine

1 9-ounce package frozen artichoke
  hearts, thawed
½ cup dry white wine *or* vermouth
½ cup chicken broth
¼ cup half-and-half *or* whipping cream
  Grated Parmesan cheese

Dust veal lightly with flour and seasonings. Sauté in butter over medium-high heat 4 to 6 minutes. Transfer to serving platter and keep warm. Add artichokes, wine, broth, and half-and-half to skillet. Cover and simmer until artichokes are tender. Pour over veal and dust with cheese.

Fresh Herbed Pasta

Makes 4 servings

2 quarts water
1 teaspoon salt
8 ounces wide fresh noodles
1 tablespoon oil

Freshly ground black pepper
2 tablespoons chopped fresh rosemary,
  thyme, *or* chives

Bring water and salt to a boil. Add noodles and oil; cook until tender but firm, 5 to 8 minutes. Drain. Toss with pepper and rosemary before serving.

Sautéed Medley

Makes 4 servings

3/4 pound small new potatoes, quartered
Water
1 teaspoon salt
1 large carrot, cut in sticks
4 small white onions, halved

2 tablespoons butter
1/2 pound mushrooms, halved
1 teaspoon lemon juice
1 teaspoon dried basil
Grated Parmesan, Romano, *or* Sapsago cheese, optional

In a large kettle cover potatoes with water; add salt and boil until tender, about 10 minutes. After 5 minutes, add carrots and onions. Melt butter in a large skillet; sauté mushrooms. Drain boiled vegetables and sauté briefly with mushrooms. Add lemon juice and basil; toss to mix. Garnish with cheese, if desired.

Chilled Watercress Soup

Makes 4 servings

2 tablespoons butter
1 bunch green onions, chopped
2 tablespoons all-purpose flour
2 tablespoons nonfat dry milk
1 quart half-and-half, at room temperature
2 bunches watercress, roughly chopped (reserve 4 sprigs for garnish)

1/4 teaspoon nutmeg
2 teaspoons lemon juice
Salt and pepper to taste
Yogurt
Lemon slices

Melt butter in saucepan; sauté onion briefly. Stir in flour and dry milk; blend and cook until bubbly. Gradually add half-and-half. Cook, stirring continuously, until soup comes to a boil and thickens. Reduce heat; simmer. Add watercress, nutmeg, and lemon juice. Cover and simmer 3 minutes. Remove soup from heat and whirl in blender until smooth. Season to taste and chill. Garnish each serving with yogurt, a watercress sprig, and lemon slice.

Avocado Dip with Vegetables
Golden Cauliflower
Greek Stir-Fry
Pine Nut Pilaf

Avocado Dip with Vegetables

Makes approximately 1 cup

1 avocado, peeled and seeded	1 teaspoon lemon juice
1/3 cup sour cream	Dash garlic salt
2 tablespoons Italian salad dressing	1 to 2 tablespoons milk

In a bowl mash avocado, using a fork. Stir in sour cream, salad dressing, lemon juice, and garlic salt; add milk until of dipping consistency. Serve with crisp relishes.

Pine Nut Pilaf

Makes 4 servings

1 tablespoon olive oil *or* vegetable oil	2¼ cup chicken broth
1 medium red onion, minced	¼ cup lemon juice
2 to 3 garlic cloves, minced	1 to 2 tablespoons chopped fresh mint
1¼ cups long-grain rice	Freshly grated rind of 1 lemon
1/3 cup pine nuts *or* slivered almonds	Freshly ground pepper

Heat oil in a medium saucepan over medium-high heat. Add onion and garlic; sauté until soft, about 5 minutes. Add rice and nuts; stir until golden brown. Add broth and lemon juice; bring to a boil. Reduce heat; cover and simmer until liquid is absorbed, 20 to 25 minutes. Just before serving, add mint, lemon rind, and pepper; fluff with two forks.

Avocado Dip with Vegetables, this page

Greek Stir-Fry

Makes 4 servings

1 tablespoon olive oil *or* vegetable oil
1 pound lamb, cubed (leg, shoulder, or shank)
1 red onion, diced
2 to 3 cloves garlic, minced
1 cup red wine
1 cup beef broth
¼ cup minced fresh parsley
1 to 2 teaspoons chopped fresh mint *or* parsley
1 teaspoon oregano
1 small eggplant, diced
1 teaspoon arrowroot, optional
Sliced black olives
Parsley *or* mint

Heat oil in a wok or skillet. Add lamb, onion, and garlic; sauté until lamb is browned. Deglaze wok with wine. Add broth, parsley, mint, and oregano; simmer about 25 minutes. Add eggplant during the last 10 minutes of cooking time. Reduce liquid over high heat or thicken by stirring in arrowroot, if desired. Garnish with olives and sprinkle with parsley.

Golden Cauliflower

Makes 4 servings

2 tablespoons butter *or* margarine
4 cups thinly sliced cauliflower
⅓ cup water
1 cup shredded Cheddar cheese
1 teaspoon paprika

Melt butter *or* margarine in large skillet; add cauliflower and water. Cover and steam over high heat for 3 minutes. Sprinkle with cheese and paprika; cover and continue steaming until cheese melts and cauliflower is tender, about 2 minutes.

Menus Extras: Dessert

Layered Fruits with Citrus-Honey Ricotta

Makes 4 servings

1 cup ricotta cheese
1 cup cream cheese
  Grated rind of 1 lemon
  Grated rind of 1 orange
  Grated rind of 1 lime
1 to 2 tablespoons lemon juice
1 to 2 tablespoons orange juice

1 to 2 tablespoons lime juice
¼ cup honey
2 to 3 tablespoons fresh chopped mint, optional
  Sliced fresh fruits (berries, bananas, plums, peaches)
  Fresh mint leaves, optional

Combine cheeses, fruit zest, honey, and chopped mint, if desired; blend well. Layer mixture with sliced fruit in parfait glasses. Chill before serving. Garnish with fresh mint sprigs.

Bananas with Rum Cream

Makes 4 servings

1 egg, separated
¼ cup brown sugar
½ of a 4-ounce container frozen whipped dessert topping, thawed

1 tablespoon dark rum
4 small bananas, sliced
  Chocolate curls, optional

In a small mixer bowl beat egg white until soft peaks form; gradually add half of the brown sugar, beating until stiff peaks form. Transfer to a clean bowl. In the same mixer bowl, beat egg yolk until thick and lemon-colored; beat in remaining brown sugar and rum. Fold egg white and dessert topping into yolk mixture. Chill until serving time. To serve, place sliced bananas in 4 dessert dishes. Spoon rum cream over fruit. Garnish with choclate curls, if desired.

Hot Fruit Compote

Makes 4 servings

½ cup dry white wine, champagne, *or* sparkling cider
1 tablespoon brown sugar, optional
¼ teaspoon ginger
¼ teaspoon nutmeg
¼ teaspoon cinnamon
½ thinly sliced lemon *or* lime
4 small peaches, apples, *or* 2 fresh pears, sliced

Combine all ingredients except fruit in a saucepan and bring to a boil. Reduce heat. Add fruit; cook and stir occasionally until tender, about 10 minutes. Serve warm.

Fresh Fruit Gelati

Makes 1 quart

2 ripe bananas
2 ripe papayas
1 tablespoon orange juice
1 tablespoon lemon juice
1 tablespoon lime juice
1 tablespoon grated orange rind
1 tablespoon grated lemon rind
1 tablespoon grated lime rind
4 cups milk
½ cup sugar
1 teaspoon vanilla

Combine all ingredients in food processor. Process until blended. Transfer to shallow cake pan and freeze overnight. Process again until smooth. Transfer to bowl and freeze overnight again. Serve with cookies or fresh fruit slices.

Variations

Rhubarb-Strawberry Gelati: Replace bananas and papayas with 2½ cups *each* sliced rhubarb and trimmed strawberries. Add additional sugar to taste.

Pineapple-Kiwi Gelati: Replace bananas and papayas with 1 very ripe peeled and chopped pineapple plus 4 kiwi fruits, peeled and diced.

Fresh Fruit Gelati, this page

Index